Understanding

A Comprehensive Guide for Executors, Heirs,
and Families

Dr. Biller Sommers

Table of Content

1st Chapter

What Exactly Is Probate?

Probate is a legal process that takes place after a person dies. It entails formalizing and administering their estate, which includes their assets, properties, debts, and other financial affairs.

The primary goals of probate are to ensure that the deceased's debts are settled, their assets are distributed according to their wishes (if a valid will exists), and any disputes among heirs or beneficiaries are resolved in a transparent and orderly manner.

This process is usually overseen by a court and carried out by an executor or administrator who is in charge of managing and distributing the assets by applicable laws and regulations. Probate laws and procedures differ from jurisdiction to jurisdiction.

Why is Probate Required?

Probate is required for several important reasons:

1. Legal Confirmation: It ensures that the document meets legal requirements and provides official recognition of the validity of a person's will (if one exists).

2. Asset Protection: Probate protects the deceased's assets during the transition period, ensuring that they are properly managed and distributed.

3. Creditor Notification: It enables a structured process for notifying and settling any outstanding debts or claims against the estate of the deceased.

4. Dispute Resolution: Probate provides a formal forum for resolving disagreements between heirs, beneficiaries, or potential

claimants. It establishes clear ownership rights and facilitates the transfer of title for assets such as real estate or investments.

5. Legal Accountability: The probate process ensures that the executor or administrator follows the law, protecting the interests of all parties involved.

6. Prevents Undue Influence or Exploitation of Vulnerable Heirs: It provides oversight to prevent any undue influence or exploitation of vulnerable heirs, particularly minors or individuals with diminished capacity.

7. Public Record: Probate proceedings are public records, which can aid in maintaining transparency and accountability in asset distribution.

While probate is a necessary legal process, it is important to note that in some cases, individuals may use strategies to reduce the impact of probate, such as establishing trusts or designating beneficiaries on specific accounts or assets. Individuals can navigate this process more effectively by consulting with legal professionals.

Who are the main characters?
The following are typical key players in the probate process:

1. Decedent: A person who has died and whose estate is being probated.

2. Executor: The person or entity named by the decedent (as specified in their will) or appointed by the court to oversee the probate process. Their responsibilities include asset gathering and management, debt settlement, and asset distribution to heirs or beneficiaries.

3. Administrator: If there is no valid will, or if the named executor is unable or unwilling to

serve, the court may appoint an administrator to perform the duties of an executor.

4. Heirs/Beneficiaries: Individuals or entities named in the will (beneficiaries) or those entitled to inherit under intestacy laws (heirs).

5. Creditor(s): Any individual or entity to whom the decedent owed money. They have the right to file claims against the estate to be reimbursed.

6. Probate Court: The legal authority in charge of overseeing the probate process, ensuring compliance with applicable laws, and resolving any disputes.

7. Attorney: Legal professionals who assist with the probate process by providing legal advice, preparing and filing necessary documents, and, if necessary, representing the executor or administrator in court.

8. Appraiser: A professional who determines the value of assets such as real estate, valuable collectibles, or businesses.

9. Accountant: An accountant may be hired in some cases to handle financial matters, particularly if the estate is complex or involves significant financial assets.

10. Witnesses: People who can attest to the will's validity, if one exists. In the probate process, their testimony may be required.

11. Guardian ad Litem: In cases involving minors or individuals with diminished capacity, the court may appoint a guardian ad Litem to represent their interests.

These key players collaborate to navigate the probate process, ensuring that the deceased's wishes are carried out, debts are settled, and assets are appropriately distributed.

2nd Chapter

Initiating the Probate Process

Starting the probate process entails several critical steps:

1. Find and secure the decedent's last will: The first step is to locate and secure the decedent's last will. This document outlines their asset distribution wishes.

2. File a Petition: If there is no will, the appointed executor (or an interested party) must file a petition with the probate court in the jurisdiction where the deceased person lived. This petition formally requests that the probate process be initiated.

3. Notify Heirs and Beneficiaries: The probate proceedings should be notified to all known heirs and beneficiaries, as well as any individuals named in the will.

4. Notify Creditors: In many cases, a notice in a local newspaper is required to notify potential creditors of the probate proceedings. This provides them with the opportunity to file claims against the estate.

5. Inventory Assets and Properties: It is the executor's responsibility to identify, catalog, and value all of the decedent's assets. Real estate, financial accounts, personal belongings, and any other valuable items are all included.

6. Establish Executor's Authority: The court will issue an order granting the executor legal authority over the estate. This document is required for tasks such as accessing bank accounts or selling real estate.

7. Open a Bank Account for the Estate: A separate bank account should be opened to manage estate funds. This account will be used to handle expenses, debt payments, and asset distribution.

8. Notify Creditors and Settle Debts: The executor must notify known creditors and allow them to file claims against the estate. Debts should be paid with assets from the estate.

9. Manage and Maintain Estate Assets: Throughout the probate process, the executor is responsible for safeguarding and managing the estate assets. This could include tasks like property maintenance, investment management, or handling rental income.

10. Prepare and File Tax Returns: The estate may be subject to various taxes, such as income and estate taxes. The executor must ensure that all required tax returns are correctly prepared and filed.

Initiating the probate process is a critical first step in settling a deceased person's affairs. It lays the groundwork for their estate's systematic and legal administration.

Obtaining Required Documents

Gathering the necessary documents for the probate process is an important step in ensuring the estate's smooth and efficient administration.

Here is a list of commonly required documents:

1. Last will: This document outlines the deceased person's wishes for asset distribution. If a will exists, it is an important part of the probate process.

2. Death Certificate: A certified copy of the death certificate is required to begin probate proceedings. It serves as official confirmation of the decedent's death.

3. Assets and liabilities list: A comprehensive inventory of the decedent's assets, including real estate, financial accounts, personal property, and any outstanding debts or liabilities.

4. Property Deeds: Documents that establish real estate property ownership, such as deeds, titles, and mortgage documents.

5. Bank Statements and Financial Records: All bank statements, investment statements, retirement accounts, and other financial holdings.

6. Insurance Policies: Documents about life insurance policies, such as policy details, beneficiaries, and insurance company contact information.

7. Retirement Accounts and Pension Plans: Details on any retirement accounts or pension plans, such as account numbers, balances, and beneficiaries.

8. Business Ownership Documents: Relevant documents such as partnership agreements, corporate records, or operating agreements if the deceased person owned a business.

9. Estate Tax Returns (if applicable): Copies of any previous estate tax returns if the deceased person was subject to estate tax in the past.

10. Outstanding Bills and Debts: Documentation of the deceased's outstanding bills, loans, mortgages, or other debts.

11. Beneficiary Designation Proof: Any documents that name beneficiaries for accounts or assets that pass outside of probate, such as payable-on-death (POD) accounts or transfer-on-death (TOD) designations.

12. Marriage and Divorce Certificates: Documents relating to the deceased's marital history, such as marriage certificates, divorce decrees, or separation agreements, if applicable.

13. Guardianship or Custody Documents (if applicable): Documents about minor children's guardianship or custody, if applicable.

14. Powers of Attorney or Healthcare Directives: Documents indicating any powers of attorney or healthcare directives executed by the deceased.

15. Trust Documents: If the deceased person established any trusts, including revocable living trusts, the trust documents are essential for understanding how these assets will be handled.

Petition Submission

The filing of the petition is a critical step in starting the probate process. This is how it's done:

1. Prepare the Petition: The appointed executor (or an interested party if there is no will) should

draft the petition with the assistance of an attorney. This document formally requests that the probate proceedings be initiated.

2. Include Required Information: Identify the decedent by name and provide the date of death.
   - State the petitioner's relationship to the decedent as well as their stake in the estate.
   - Indicate whether the decedent had a valid will and attach a copy if so.

3. File with Probate Court: Submit the completed petition to the probate court in the jurisdiction where the deceased person resided at the time of death.

4. Pay the Filing Fee: The petition may be subject to a filing fee. This varies depending on the jurisdiction.

5. Request Letters Testamentary or Letters of Administration: In addition to the petition, the petitioner will typically request that the court issue either Letters Testamentary (if a valid will

exists) or Letters of Administration (if no valid will exists).

6. Notify Heirs and Beneficiaries: Make certain that all known heirs and beneficiaries are notified of the start of probate proceedings.

7. Publication of a Notice to Creditors (if required): Depending on local laws, a notice to creditors may be required to be published in a local newspaper to inform potential claimants of the probate process.

8. Attend Court Hearings (if necessary): The court may schedule a hearing to review the petition in some cases. As needed, the petitioner or their attorney should appear.

9. Obtain a Court Order Granting Authority: Once the court has reviewed and approved the petition, it will issue an order formally appointing the executor or administrator and granting them the legal authority to act on behalf of the estate.

The filing of the petition formally initiates the probate process, laying the groundwork for the systematic administration of the deceased person's estate. It's an important step because it establishes the legal framework for managing and distributing assets by the law and the deceased's wishes.

Nomination of an Executor

The appointment of an executor is a major step in the probate process. This is how it usually goes:

1. Will Nomination: If the deceased person had a valid will, they most likely named an executor in it. This person has been nominated as the executor's first choice.

2. Acceptance of Nomination: The executor who has been nominated must accept the responsibility. If they choose to decline, an alternate executor may be named in the will.

3. Petition for Appointment: If there is no valid will, the nominated executor (or an interested party) files a petition with the probate court to formally request appointment as the executor.

4. Court Review and Approval: The petition will be reviewed by the court, and a hearing may be scheduled to ensure that the nominated executor is qualified and willing to take on the role.

5. Alternatives Considered: If the nominated executor is unable or unwilling to serve, or if no valid will exists, the court may consider appointing an administrator. This person performs similar duties but is appointed by the court rather than nominated by the deceased.

6. Factors to Consider When Choosing an Executor:
   - Capacity: The executor must be of legal age and mentally capable of handling the responsibilities.

- Conflict of Interest: The court will consider whether the executor has any conflicts of interest that could impair his or her ability to act impartially.

- Prior Experience: Prior experience or familiarity with legal and financial matters is advantageous, but not always required.

7. Official Appointment: Once approved, the court will issue an order naming the executor and granting them legal authority to act on behalf of the estate.

8. Receive Letters Testamentary: If the will is valid, the executor will be given "Letters Testamentary." This is a legal document that proves their right to manage the estate.

9. Notify Interested Parties: The executor should notify all interested parties about their appointment, including heirs, beneficiaries, and creditors.

The appointment of the executor is a critical step because this person will be in charge of managing and overseeing the probate process. They are in charge of gathering assets, settling debts, and distributing remaining assets by the deceased's wishes or as required by applicable laws. The executor must approach their duties with care, diligence, and by legal requirements.

3rd Chapter

Asset Inventory and Appraisal

The inventory and appraisal of assets is a critical component of the probate process. This is how it is usually done:

1. **Document Gathering:** The executor begins by gathering all relevant documents pertaining to the deceased's assets. This includes bank statements, property deeds, investment records, and any other paperwork that is relevant.

2. **Physical Inspection**: A physical inspection is often required to determine the condition and value of tangible assets such as real estate, vehicles, jewelry, and valuable personal belongings.

3. **Hiring Professionals (if Necessary):** In some cases, hiring professionals such as appraisers, real estate agents, or financial advisors may be

necessary to accurately assess the value of certain assets.

4. **Determining Fair Market Value:** Assets should be appraised at their fair market value, or the price at which they would sell on the open market. This is essential for proper accounting and distribution.

5. **Valuing Intangible Assets**: Valuation of intangible assets such as intellectual property, copyrights, trademarks, or business interests may necessitate specialized knowledge.

6. **Asset Documentation**: The executor compiles a detailed list of all assets, including their description, estimated value, and any accompanying documentation. This inventory should be comprehensive and well-documented. Appraisers or professionals involved in the valuation process should provide certificates or reports detailing their assessments.

8. **Asset Protection**: It is critical to protect valuable assets during this process to avoid loss or damage.

9. **Dealing with Special Assets:** Some assets, such as collectibles, antiques, or rare items, may necessitate the services of specialized appraisers who are knowledgeable in those fields.

10. **Court Reporting:** The executor submits the inventory and appraisal information to the probate court. This report is usually due within a certain amount of time.

11. **Potential Difficulties:** If there are disagreements or disputes about the valuation of specific assets, the executor may need to consult with professionals or seek court approval to reach a fair resolution.

12. **Updates and revaluation (if necessary):** In some cases, assets may need to be revalued, especially if a long time has passed since the initial appraisal.

Accurate and thorough asset inventory and appraisal are critical for equitable estate distribution and compliance with legal requirements. Executors should approach this task with caution and, if necessary, seek professional assistance.

Finding Estate Assets

The identification of estate assets is an important step in the probate process. This is how it is usually done:

1. *Gather Documentation:* Begin by gathering all relevant financial documents pertaining to the deceased. This includes bank statements, investment records, property deeds, and any other documentation pertaining to their assets.

2. *Examine Personal Records*: Look for any additional information about the decedent's

assets in their personal records, such as files, safes, or digital storage.

3. *Investigate Financial Accounts:* Examine bank statements, brokerage accounts, retirement accounts, and any other financial records for balances, holdings, and account numbers.

4. *Investigate Real Estate Holdings:* Gather information on any real estate that the deceased owned. This includes residential and commercial properties, as well as land and any associated mortgages or liens.

5. *Inventory Valuable Personal Belongings:* Make a list of valuable personal belongings such as jewelry, artwork, antiques, collectibles, and household items. These can be quite valuable.

6. *Examine Business Interests:* Gather information about the deceased's ownership interests in businesses, partnerships, or sole proprietorships.

7. *Examine Life Insurance Policies*: Look for any life insurance policies and collect information such as policy numbers, beneficiaries, and coverage amounts.

8. *Examine Retirement and Pension Plans:* Determine whether the deceased had any retirement accounts, pensions, or annuities, and collect information on account numbers and beneficiaries.

9. *Look for Digital Assets:* In this day and age, it's critical to think about online accounts, cryptocurrencies, and other digital assets. Email accounts, social media profiles, and online financial platforms are examples.

10. *Verify Vehicles and Other Tangible Assets:* Collect information on vehicles, boats, recreational vehicles, and other tangible assets. This includes titles and registration documents.

11. *Consider Intellectual Property and Royalties:* Investigate any intellectual property,

such as patents, trademarks, copyrights, or royalties from creative works, if applicable.

12. *Examine your debts and liabilities*: Along with assets, any outstanding debts, mortgages, loans, or other financial obligations must be identified.

13. *Consult Professionals*: If the deceased had a financial advisor, accountant, or attorney, they can be invaluable resources for determining the extent of the estate's assets.

A thorough and efficient probate process requires accurate asset identification. It serves as the foundation for compiling an inventory, determining their value, and ultimately distributing them in accordance with the wishes of the decedent or applicable laws.

Asset Assessment

The valuation of assets is an important step in the probate process. This is how it is usually done:

1. Hire Professionals (if necessary): When dealing with complex or high-value assets, it's often a good idea to hire professionals such as appraisers, real estate agents, or financial advisors. They are capable of providing accurate and unbiased assessments.

2. Fair Market Value: The fair market value of assets should be determined. This is the price at which the asset would sell on the open market if there were a willing buyer and seller.

3. Real Estate: The fair market value of real estate can be determined by a professional appraiser or real estate agent based on factors such as location, condition, comparable sales, and market trends.

4. Tangible Personal Property: To provide accurate valuations for items such as jewelry,

artwork, antiques, and collectibles, an appraiser with expertise in those specific categories is frequently required.

5. Financial Accounts: The current balances or market values of financial accounts such as bank accounts, stocks, bonds, and retirement accounts determine their value.

6. Business Interests: Valuing business interests is a complex process that may necessitate the use of a professional business appraiser to assess factors such as revenue, assets, liabilities, and industry trends.

7. Life Insurance: The face value of a life insurance policy is typically its value. However, if the policy includes a cash value component, that may also be included.

Vehicles and Tangible Assets: The value of vehicles, boats, and other tangible assets can frequently be determined using sources such as Kelley Blue Book or by consulting with experts.

9. Debts and Liabilities: When calculating an asset's net value, subtract any outstanding debts or liabilities associated with it.

10. Special Asset Considerations: Unique or specialized assets, such as intellectual property or rare collectibles, may necessitate the services of a specialized appraiser with expertise in those fields.

11. Keep detailed records of the valuations for each asset, as well as any documentation or reports provided by professionals.

12. Revaluations (if necessary): In some cases, assets may need to be revalued, especially if a long time has passed since the initial appraisal.

Accurate asset valuation ensures that the estate's value is correctly calculated, which affects asset distribution to heirs and beneficiaries. It's critical to approach this task with caution and, when necessary, seek professional help for accurate and reliable valuations.

Process of Appraisal

The appraisal process is a systematic method for determining the value of assets. This is how it is usually done:

1. Hiring a Qualified Appraiser: A qualified appraiser is hired for assets that require professional evaluation, such as real estate, valuable art, or collectibles. It is critical to select an appraiser who is knowledgeable about the type of asset being appraised.

2. Defining the Scope of Work: The appraiser and the executor or estate representative discuss the appraisal's purpose, the type of value sought (e.g., fair market value, insurance value, etc.), and the specific assets to be appraised.

3. Inspection and Examination: The appraiser examines the asset physically, noting its

condition, size, features, and any relevant details that may affect its value.

4. Research and Analysis: The appraiser conducts extensive research on the asset, taking into account factors such as market trends, comparable sales (for real estate), provenance (for art and collectibles), and any other factors influencing value.

5. Selection of Appropriate Valuation Methods: The appraiser employs appropriate valuation methods based on the type of asset. Real estate, for example, can be valued using the sales comparison approach, the cost approach, or the income approach.

6. Documentation and Reporting: The appraiser writes a detailed report that details their findings. This report contains a description of the asset, the valuation method used, supporting data, and the final value.

7. Professional Ethics and Standards: Appraisers must follow ethical guidelines and professional standards to ensure that their work is objective, unbiased, and accurately reflects the asset's value.

8. Review and Verification: The report is checked for completeness and accuracy. Any discrepancies or missing information can be addressed at this stage.

9. Presentation to the Executor or Estate Representative: The appraiser explains the methodology used and provides the final valuation to the executor or estate representative.

10. Application in the Probate Process: The appraised value of the asset is an important piece of information in the probate process. It contributes to the overall value of the estate and informs distribution decisions to heirs or beneficiaries.

11. Document Retention: The appraisal report, as well as any supporting documentation, should be kept on file as part of the estate's documentation.

12. Potential Dispute Resolution: If there is a disagreement about the appraised value, the report and methodology can be used to back up the appraiser's findings.

The appraisal process ensures that assets are correctly and objectively valued, laying the groundwork for informed decision-making during the probate process. It is critical to select a qualified and reputable appraiser in order to obtain reliable valuations.

4th Chapter

Creditor Notification and Debt Resolution

Notifying creditors and settling debts is an important step in the probate process. This is how it is usually done:

1. Identify and Compile a Creditor List: The executor collects information about any known or potential creditors. This may include the deceased's outstanding bills, loans, mortgages, credit card debts, and any other financial obligations.

2. Publish Notice to Creditors (if required): In some jurisdictions, a notice in a local newspaper is required to inform potential creditors about the probate proceedings. This gives them a specific time frame in which to file claims against the estate.

3. Notify Known Creditors Directly: In addition to publishing a public notice, the executor should notify known creditors directly about the probate proceedings. This can be accomplished through written correspondence or by directly contacting them.

4. Claim Review and Validation: As claims are received, the executor checks them for validity. This includes confirming the debt's legitimacy and ensuring that it is properly documented.

5. Debt Prioritization: Some debts may take precedence over others. Funeral expenses and administrative costs associated with the probate process, for example, usually take precedence.

6. Dispute or Contest Invalid Claims: If the executor has concerns about the validity of a specific claim, he or she may need to address the issue directly with the creditor or seek legal advice.

7. Negotiate Settlements (if Necessary): In some cases, the executor may negotiate a settlement with creditors, especially if the estate lacks sufficient funds to cover all outstanding debts.

8. Pay Valid Debts with Estate Funds: The executor pays off valid and verified debts with estate funds. This includes any taxes that the deceased owed.

9. Keep Extensive Records: The executor keeps meticulous records of all communications with creditors, as well as documentation pertaining to the resolution of each debt.

10. File Tax Returns and Pay Taxes: It is critical to ensure that all applicable taxes are filed and paid as part of the debt resolution process.

11. Request Releases or Discharges: Once a debt has been paid, the executor may ask the creditor for a release or discharge to confirm that the debt has been settled.

12. Final Accounting: In the final stages of the probate process, the executor submits to the court for approval an accounting of all actions taken, including debt resolution.

Notifying creditors and resolving debts is an important part of probate because it ensures that the deceased's financial obligations are met before distributing assets to heirs or beneficiaries. Executors must approach this process with caution, transparency, and adherence to all applicable laws and regulations.

Notification to Creditors

A formal step in the probate process that informs potential creditors of the deceased's estate about the ongoing proceedings is the publication of a notice to creditors. This is how it is usually done:

1. Drafting the Notice: The notice should include important information such as the deceased's name, date of death, and a statement stating that

creditors must present their claims within a certain time frame.

2. Determining Publication Requirements: Each jurisdiction has different requirements for publishing a notice to creditors. It is critical to investigate and comprehend the local laws and regulations that govern this process.

3. Choosing a Publication: The notice is typically published in the local newspaper of the deceased person's residence at the time of death. The legal requirements for public notices must be met by the newspaper.

4. Contacting the Newspaper: Inquire with the chosen newspaper about their specific procedures for publishing legal notices. This may entail filing the notice and paying a fee.

5. Include the Following Information in the Notice:
- The deceased's full name
- Demise date

- The executor's or personal representative's name and contact information
- A statement stating that creditors must present their claims within a certain time frame (as required by local laws).

6. The notice is typically published for a set period of time, which is determined by local regulations. Periods can last anywhere from a few weeks to a few months.

7. Monitoring Responses: The executor or personal representative should be prepared to receive and review any claims submitted by creditors during the publication period.

8. Addressing Claims: Valid creditors' claims must be addressed in accordance with the laws and regulations that govern the probate process.

9. Keep detailed records of the publication, including copies of the published notice and any correspondence with creditors.

10. Court Documentation: To demonstrate compliance with legal requirements, the executor may be required to file proof of the published notice with the probate court in some jurisdictions.

11. Finalizing the Probate Process: Once the notice period has ended and all valid creditor claims have been addressed, the probate process can move forward with asset distribution.

The publication of a notice to creditors is an important step in ensuring that potential creditors have an opportunity to present their claims against the estate. Executors must strictly adhere to legal procedures and document all actions taken during the process.

Claim Evaluation

In a probate proceeding, claims are evaluated to determine the validity of any claims made against the deceased person's estate. This usually includes debts, expenses, and asset distribution requests. It is critical to:

1. Examine any documents that support the claim, such as invoices, contracts, or legal agreements.

2. Confirm that the claimant is a legitimate creditor or beneficiary. This could include reviewing legal documents or contracts.

3. Check for Statute of Limitations: Ensure that the claim is filed within the timeframe specified by law.

4. Determine Priority: Determine the order of claims. Certain debts or expenses may take precedence over others.

5. Examine Validity: Examine the claim's validity. Is the debt, for example, legally enforceable?

6. Consider Contingent Claims: Assess any potential or contingent claims that may arise in the future.

7. Negotiate or Dispute: If necessary, negotiate or disagree with the claimant or their representative about the claim.

8. Keep detailed records of the evaluation process and any decisions made in relation to each claim.

9. Court Approval: If local laws require it, seek court approval for distributions and payments.

Remember that specific guidance in probate matters should be sought from a qualified attorney or legal advisor, as laws and procedures vary by jurisdiction.

Resolving Unpaid Debts
In a probate proceeding, outstanding debts must be resolved in a systematic manner to ensure that

all legitimate debts are paid in full. Here are some actions you can take:

1. Make a List of Debts: Make a thorough list of all known debts owed by the deceased. Mortgages, loans, credit card balances, medical bills, and other debts may be included.

2. Confirm the legitimacy of each debt claim by verifying creditor claims. Check to see if the creditor has provided adequate documentation to back up their claim.

3. Debt Prioritization: Determine the order of debts. Some debts, such as funeral expenses or taxes, may have a higher priority.

4. Notify Creditors: Inform all known creditors of the individual's death. Give them the information they need to submit their claims.

5. Negotiate if Necessary: It may be possible to negotiate with creditors to settle debts for a lower amount in some cases.

6. Check for Insurance or Benefits: Determine whether any of the outstanding debts are covered by insurance policies or benefits, and file appropriate claims.

7. If the estate does not have enough liquid assets to cover the debts, consider selling non-essential assets to generate funds.

8. Obtain Court Approval: If required by local laws, seek court approval for debt repayment. This ensures that the distribution follows all legal procedures.

9. Maintain Extensive Records: Document all communications, payments, and agreements with creditors. This keeps a detailed record of the debt resolution process.

10. Debt Payments: Once all legitimate debts have been verified and prioritized, distribute the remaining funds as needed.

Remember to seek specific advice from a probate attorney or legal advisor, especially if the estate is complex or there are legal disputes regarding the debts. They can offer valuable insight into how to navigate the process effectively.

5th Chapter

Asset Distribution to Heirs

In a probate proceeding, distributing assets to heirs necessitates careful planning and adherence to legal procedures. Here's a step-by-step procedure:

1. Identify and Value Assets: Make a thorough inventory of all estate assets, including real estate, bank accounts, investments, personal property, and so on. If necessary, seek professional evaluations.

2. Valid Wills and Trusts: Check to see if there are any valid wills or trusts in place that specify how the assets should be distributed. Take the steps outlined in these documents.

3. Inform Heirs: Inform the heirs of their right to the estate. If applicable, provide them with copies of relevant legal documents.

4. Prior to distributing assets, settle any outstanding debts, expenses, and taxes associated with the estate.

5. Obtain Court Approval (if needed): In some cases, such as large or complex estates, court approval may be required. This ensures that legal procedures are followed.

6. Equal Distribution: If specified in the will, distribute assets in accordance with the instructions. If not, think about a just and equitable distribution among heirs.

7. Update legal titles and ownership documents for assets such as real estate, vehicles, and financial accounts to reflect the new owners.

8. Maintain detailed records of all asset distributions, including dates, descriptions, and parties involved.

9. Give Receipts or Acknowledgements: Give the heirs receipts or acknowledgements for the assets they have received. This can help to avoid future disagreements.

10. Complete the Probate Process: Once all assets have been distributed, file the necessary paperwork to end the probate process.

11. Seek Professional Advice: Consultation with a probate attorney or legal advisor is recommended, especially in complex cases. They can advise you on legal requirements and help you navigate any potential snags.

Remember that laws and procedures vary by jurisdiction, so it's critical to follow local regulations. When dealing with probate matters, always seek professional legal advice.

If applicable, interpreting the Will

The interpretation of a will is an important step in the probate process. It entails determining the deceased's intentions regarding the distribution of their assets. Here's how you can go about it:

1. Carefully read the will: Begin by thoroughly reading the will. Take note of the language used and any specific instructions given.

2. Determine who the named beneficiaries are and what assets or properties are allocated to each of them.

3. Clarify Ambiguities: Seek legal advice to help interpret any unclear or ambiguous terms in the will. This is critical in order to avoid potential conflicts.

4. Examine Residuary Clauses: Look for a residuary clause that specifies how any remaining assets or properties should be distributed.

5. Contingencies should be considered: Look for provisions that address what happens if a beneficiary outlives the testator (the person who wrote the will).

6. Understanding Specific Bequests: Pay close attention to specific bequests, which are items or amounts designated for specific beneficiaries. Make certain that these are clearly identified.

7. Check for Conditions or Restrictions: Determine whether the bequests are subject to any conditions or restrictions, such as age requirements or other criteria.

8. Examine the Executor's Powers: Examine the executor's powers and responsibilities to ensure they are consistent with the provisions in the will.

9. Consult with Legal Professionals: If the will contains complex or contentious provisions, seek the advice of a probate attorney or legal advisor.

10. Communicate with Beneficiaries: Once you've interpreted the will, make its provisions clear and transparent to the beneficiaries.

11. Keep detailed records of the steps taken to interpret the will during the interpretation process. This can be useful in the event of future disputes.

Remember that interpreting a will should be done with great care and, if necessary, with the assistance of a legal professional to ensure accuracy and compliance with legal requirements.

Intestate Succession (in the absence of a Will)

Intestate succession occurs when a person dies without leaving a valid will. In such cases, state law governs the distribution of the deceased's assets.

The following is a general overview of how intestate succession typically works:

1. Determine Legal Heirs: The first step is to identify the legal heirs. Depending on the jurisdiction, this usually includes the surviving spouse, children, parents, and, in some cases, siblings or more distant relatives.

2. Distribute to Spouse and Children: In many jurisdictions, the primary heirs are the surviving spouse and children. Depending on local laws, they may inherit the estate in various proportions.

3. Spouse's Share: Typically, the surviving spouse receives a substantial portion of the estate, often as a percentage or, in some cases, the entire estate.

4. Children's Share: If there are children, they usually receive the remainder of the estate. Depending on the jurisdiction, the distribution of children may differ.

5. Other Family Members: If no surviving spouse or children exist, the estate may pass to parents, siblings, or more distant relatives under intestate succession laws.

6. Follow State Laws: Each state has its own set of laws that govern how assets are distributed in intestate situations. Certain relatives are given preference over others under these laws.

7. Account for Adopted and Stepchildren: Adopted and stepchildren are often treated the same as biological children for intestate succession purposes.

8. Addressing Half-Siblings: Half-sibling laws vary. Some jurisdictions treat them the same as full siblings, while others do not.

9. Keep detailed records of the determination of legal heirs to document and validate heirship. This documentation may be required to transfer assets legally.

10. Seek Legal Advice: Due to the complexities of intestate succession laws and potential family dynamics, it is best to seek advice from a probate attorney or legal advisor.

It's important to note that intestate succession laws can vary significantly from one jurisdiction to the next, so it's critical to follow the specific laws in the relevant area. In intestate cases, consulting with a legal professional is highly recommended to ensure compliance with local regulations.

Transferring Property

The legal process of transferring ownership from one party to another is referred to as asset transfer. Here's a general guide to getting started:

1. Identify the Asset: Make a clear identification of the asset you wish to transfer. This includes real estate, financial accounts, personal property, and so on.

2. Verify Ownership and Title: Make sure you have legal ownership or authority over the asset you're about to transfer.

3. Examine the Legal Requirements: Learn about the legal requirements for transferring a specific type of asset. Different procedures may apply to different types of assets.

4. Think about the Recipient: Figure out who will receive the asset and confirm their willingness to accept it.

5. Select a Transfer Method:
- Sale: If the asset is being transferred for monetary value, consider selling it. Negotiating a fair price, drafting a contract, and facilitating the transfer of funds are all part of this process.
Gift: If you transfer an asset without expecting anything in return, you may be gifting it. This could have tax consequences, so be aware of gift tax laws.

- Inheritance: As part of the probate process, assets of a deceased person may be transferred to heirs or beneficiaries.

- Joint Ownership: You can add a co-owner to some assets, such as bank accounts or real estate. This can make the transfer process easier.

6. Complete the following documentation:
- Deeds: When selling real estate, you must prepare and sign a deed transferring ownership to the new owner.
- Contracts: When selling an asset, draft a contract outlining the terms of the transaction.

- Gift Letters: If you are gifting an asset, consider providing a written statement confirming your intention to do so.

7. Obtain Professional Help:
- Legal Counsel: Consult a lawyer for advice, especially on complex transfers or assets with legal complexities.

- Financial Advisor: They can advise on the financial consequences of asset transfers.

- Real Estate Agent: If you are transferring real estate, you should consider hiring a real estate agent to handle the paperwork.

8. Submit Any Required Documents: Submit any required documents to the appropriate authorities, such as the county clerk's office for real estate transfers.

9. Keep detailed records of the transfer process, including all relevant documents and communications.

10. Notify All Relevant Parties: Notify all parties involved in the transfer, such as banks, government agencies, or other stakeholders.

Remember that asset transfer laws and procedures can vary greatly depending on the type of asset and your jurisdiction. Seeking professional advice and adhering to legal protocols are critical for a smooth and legally valid transfer.

6th Chapter

Dealing with Estate Taxes

Estate taxes are an important aspect of estate administration. Here are some actions you can take to address this issue:

1. Determine the Applicable Laws: Learn about the estate tax laws in the jurisdiction where the deceased person lived. The thresholds, exemptions, and tax rates vary by region.

2. Calculate the total value of the estate, which includes real estate, financial accounts, personal property, investments, and any other assets.

3. Identify Exemptions and Deductions*: Learn about any exemptions or deductions that may be available to reduce the taxable value of the estate. Funeral expenses, debts, and certain administrative costs are examples of common deductions.

4. Complete and submit the necessary tax forms to the appropriate tax authority. This frequently includes a federal estate tax return (such as IRS Form 706 in the United States) as well as state-level forms, if applicable.

5. Appraise Assets: Professionally appraise certain assets to determine their fair market value. This is especially true for valuable items such as real estate, art, or collectibles.

6. Consider Marital Deductions: In some jurisdictions, assets passing to a surviving spouse may be eligible for a marital deduction, lowering the taxable estate.

7. Use Credit Shelter Trusts (if applicable): Depending on the jurisdiction and the size of the estate, using trusts to maximize available exemptions may be beneficial.

8. Pay Estimated Taxes (if Required): If estimated tax payments are due before the final

tax return is filed, make them. This helps to avoid underpayment penalties.

9. Seek Professional Help: Speak with a qualified tax advisor or estate planning attorney who is familiar with local tax laws. They can offer specific advice and assist in navigating complex situations.

10. File Tax Returns on Time: Make certain that all required tax returns are filed by the deadlines. Penalties and interest charges may be imposed for late filing.

11. Settling Tax Liability: Once the tax liability has been determined, make arrangements for payment. This could include selling assets, using liquid funds from the estate, or implementing other planning strategies.

12. Maintain Extensive Records: Keep meticulous records of all estate tax-related transactions, communications, and documents.

This documentation is necessary for auditing and legal purposes.

Remember that estate tax laws and procedures are complicated and subject to change. To ensure compliance and minimize tax liability, it is critical to seek professional advice and stay up to date on current regulations.

Recognizing Estate Taxation

The process of levying taxes on the transfer of an individual's assets after death is referred to as estate taxation. Here are some key points to consider when learning about estate taxation:

1. The taxable estate consists of all assets owned by the deceased individual at the time of their death. This includes real estate, financial accounts, personal property, investments, and other assets.

2. Exemptions and Deductions: Most jurisdictions offer exemptions and deductions

that can be used to reduce the taxable value of an estate. Allowances for funeral expenses, debts, administrative costs, and specific bequests may be included.

3. Estate Tax Exemptions: Each jurisdiction has a defined exemption amount, also known as the "exemption amount" or "estate tax exclusion," below which no estate tax is owed. If the estate's value is less than this amount, it is not subject to estate taxation.

4. Tax Rates: When an estate exceeds the exemption amount, a tax rate is applied to the portion of the estate's value that exceeds the threshold. Tax rates differ greatly depending on the jurisdiction.

5. Marital Deduction: Assets passing to a surviving spouse are frequently eligible for a marital deduction in many jurisdictions. This means they are not subject to estate tax when the first spouse dies.

6. Exemption Portability: A surviving spouse in some countries, such as the United States, may be able to use any unused portion of their deceased spouse's estate tax exemption. This is referred to as "portability."

7. Considerations for Gift Taxes: Some jurisdictions impose a separate gift tax on transfers of assets made during a person's lifetime. Gift and estate taxes are frequently intertwined, with lifetime gifts potentially affecting the taxable estate.

8. Assets transferred to grandchildren or more distant descendants may be subject to an additional tax known as the generation-skipping transfer tax in certain circumstances.

9. State-Level Estate Taxes: In addition to federal or state-level estate taxes, some areas may have their own estate tax legislation. These can differ in terms of exemption amounts and tax rates.

10. Estate Tax Planning: Estate tax planning can help to reduce the impact of estate taxes. This may include strategies such as trusts, gifting, and other tax-efficient asset distribution methods.

11. Given the complexities of estate tax laws, it is strongly advised to seek the advice of a qualified tax advisor or estate planning attorney. They can give you personalized advice based on your specific circumstances and local laws.

Keep in mind that estate tax laws can be complicated and change over time. It is critical to stay informed and consult with professionals when navigating this aspect of estate planning and administration.

Returning Estate Taxes
Filing estate tax returns is a critical step in settling a deceased person's estate's tax obligations. Here's a general guide to getting started:

1. Determine the Obligation: Determine whether the estate is subject to estate taxes. This is determined by the jurisdiction as well as the total value of the estate.

2. Obtain the Required Forms: Obtain the necessary estate tax return forms from the appropriate tax authority. The primary form in the United States, for example, is IRS Form 706.

3. Collect All Relevant Financial and Asset-Related Information: Gather all relevant financial and asset-related information, including appraisals, valuations, and supporting documents.

4. Complete the Return: Fill out the estate tax return completely and accurately. Provide detailed information about the decedent, his or her assets, deductions, exemptions, and any other relevant information.

5. Attach any necessary documentation, such as appraisals, deeds, valuations, or legal

documents, that support the information provided in the return.

6. Calculate Tax Liability: Calculate the total tax liability by applying the applicable tax rates to the estate's taxable value.

7. Exemptions and Deductions: Use any available exemptions, deductions, or credits to reduce the estate's taxable value.

8. Consider the Marital Deduction and Portability (if applicable): If applicable, use the marital deduction for assets passing to a surviving spouse and consider portability of the deceased spouse's unused exemption.

9. Check and double-check the completed return to ensure accuracy and compliance with tax laws.

10. Sign and Date the Return: The estate tax return must be signed and dated by the executor or personal representative.

11. File the Return: Submit the completed return to the appropriate tax authority, along with any required documentation. Ensure that it is submitted by the jurisdiction's deadline.

12. Pay any Taxes Due: If the estate owes taxes, make arrangements for payment in accordance with the jurisdiction's rules.

13. Request an Extension (if Necessary): Consider requesting an extension if more time is required to gather information or complete the return. Make certain to complete this before the original filing deadline.

14. Maintain Thorough Records: Keep detailed records of all documents related to the filing of the estate tax return. Copies of the return, supporting documents, and any correspondence with tax authorities are all included.

15. Seek Professional Advice: Due to the complexities of estate tax laws, it is strongly

recommended that you seek the advice of a qualified tax advisor or estate planning attorney for guidance and to ensure compliance with local regulations.

Keep in mind that estate tax laws and procedures differ by jurisdiction, so it's critical to follow the specific rules in your area.

Taking Care of Tax Obligations

Fulfilling all legal requirements and making the necessary payments to the tax authorities are all part of settling tax obligations, whether for an individual or an estate. Here's a general guide to getting started:

1. Collect All Relevant Financial Documents: Gather all relevant financial documents, such as income statements, receipts, investment records, and any other documentation required for tax purposes.

2. Calculate Tax Liability: Determine the total amount of taxes owed. Income taxes, property taxes, estate taxes (if applicable), and any other applicable taxes are all included.

3. Check Deadlines: Keep track of tax filing and payment deadlines. Failure to meet deadlines may result in penalties and interest charges.

4. Fill out and submit the necessary tax forms to the appropriate tax authorities. Depending on the jurisdiction, this can be done electronically or via physical mail.

5. Pay Taxes Due: If you owe taxes, make arrangements to pay them as soon as possible. You may be able to pay online, by check, or by other accepted methods.

6. Consider Payment Plans or Extensions (if Necessary): If you are unable to pay the full amount by the deadline, contact the tax authority to discuss installment plans or a request for an extension. Keep in mind that extensions

typically provide additional time to file but not necessarily to pay.

7. Use Deductions and Credits: Use any available deductions, credits, or exemptions to reduce your tax liability. These can include mortgage interest, charitable contributions, education expenses, and other costs.

8. Consider Professional Advice: If you have a complicated tax situation or are unsure about certain deductions or credits, you should consult a qualified tax advisor or accountant.

9. Keep detailed records of all tax-related documents, such as tax returns, receipts, statements, and correspondence with tax authorities. This documentation can be useful in the event of an audit or a dispute.

10. Respond to Notices: If you receive any notices or communications from tax authorities, please respond as soon as possible. Ignoring them may result in additional complications.

11. Keep Up to Date: Stay informed about any changes in tax laws or regulations that may affect your tax situation.

12. Monitor Refunds (if applicable): If you are entitled to a tax refund, keep track of its status and ensure that it is properly deposited or issued.

13. If you discover an error or omitted information on a previously filed return, you may need to file an amended return to correct it.

Keep in mind that tax laws and procedures vary by jurisdiction and can be complicated. Seeking professional advice, particularly for complex or large financial issues, can help ensure compliance and optimize your tax situation.

7th Chapter

Putting Disputes and Controversies to Rest

Disputes and controversies, whether legal, personal, or business-related, necessitate careful consideration and effective communication. Here are some actions you can take:

1. Maintain Open Communication: Create a channel of communication between all parties involved. Make certain that all points of view are heard and understood.

2. Seek Mediation or Alternative Dispute Resolution (ADR): Consider bringing in a neutral third party to facilitate discussions and assist in reaching a mutually acceptable resolution. A neutral advisor can be a mediator, arbitrator, or both.

3. Define the Issues Clearly: Identify the specific points of contention and clarify all parties' underlying concerns.

4. Investigate Legal Options: If the dispute is particularly complex or cannot be resolved amicably, consider seeking legal counsel. Consult with a lawyer who specializes in the subject matter.

5. Encourage a spirit of compromise and negotiation. Look for solutions that are mutually beneficial and address the interests of all parties.

6. Agreements Should Be Documented: If a resolution is reached, the terms should be clearly documented in a legally binding agreement. This will help to avoid future misunderstandings.

7. Understand Legal Rights and Responsibilities: Become acquainted with all parties' legal rights and responsibilities. This can be useful context for negotiations.

8. Consider Expert Opinions: In cases where technical expertise is required (e.g., financial disputes, construction issues), consult with professionals who are knowledgeable about the subject.

9. Maintain Deadlines and Commitments: If agreements are reached, make certain that all parties fulfill their obligations on time. This increases trust and credibility.

10. Maintain a Calm and Professional Attitude: Emotions can run high during disagreements, but keeping a calm and professional demeanor can help facilitate productive discussions.

11. Consider the risks and benefits of pursuing legal action versus reaching a negotiated settlement. Consider the costs, time, and potential outcomes.

12. Consider a Formal Legal Process: If informal resolution methods fail, consider starting a

formal legal process, such as filing a lawsuit or going to arbitration.

13. Consult with Professionals: Seek advice from trusted professionals such as attorneys, financial advisors, or consultants who can provide valuable insights and expertise.

14. Keep detailed records of all communications, documents, and agreements related to the dispute. These records may be useful in legal proceedings or for future reference.

Remember that each dispute is unique, and the approach to resolution will differ depending on the circumstances. Seeking professional advice, particularly in legal matters, is frequently necessary to protect your rights and interests.

Will Competitions

When someone challenges the validity or terms of a deceased person's will, this is known as a will contest. This can be a complicated legal procedure that typically includes the following steps:

1. Grounds for Contest: The contestant must have valid legal grounds for contesting the will. Lack of testamentary capacity, undue influence, fraud, duress, or improper execution are all common grounds.

2. Consult an Attorney: The contestant should seek the advice of an experienced probate or estate attorney who can evaluate the case, explain the legal process, and guide them through the steps.

3. Filing a Petition: The contestant files a formal petition with the probate court to contest the will, often through the assistance of an attorney. This petition explains the grounds for the contest and asks the court to intervene.

4. Notification of Interested Parties: The court typically requires notification of the contest to

all interested parties, including beneficiaries named in the will and potential heirs.

5. Gathering Evidence: The contestant and their lawyer collect evidence to back up their claims. Medical records, witness testimony, financial documents, and other relevant information may be included.

6. Responding to the Contest: The executor of the estate, as well as any other interested parties, will be able to respond to the contest and present their own evidence supporting the will's validity.

7. Mediation or Settlement (Optional): In some cases, the parties may try to reach an agreement or resolve the dispute through mediation, potentially avoiding a full-fledged court battle.

8. Pre-Trial Motions and Discovery: Both parties may file motions with the court, and there may be a period of discovery during which information is exchanged.

9. Hearing in Probate Court: The court will hold a hearing to consider the evidence presented by both parties. The judge will decide whether the will is valid and enforceable at this point.

10. Judgment and Order: Based on the evidence presented, the court will issue a judgment. This judgment will decide whether the will is valid and, if necessary, outline the distribution of assets.

11. If one of the parties is dissatisfied with the court's decision, they may be able to file an appeal.

12. Final Distribution: Once all legal issues have been resolved, the estate can begin the final distribution of assets in accordance with the court's order.

Will contests can be emotionally and legally complex, and they frequently require significant time and resources. Consultation with an experienced attorney is essential for successfully navigating the process. They can provide customized advice based on the facts of the case.

Disputes Between Heirs

Disputes among heirs can be both emotionally and legally taxing. When faced with such a situation, consider the following steps:

1. Open Communication: Encourage all parties involved to communicate openly and honestly. This can aid in determining the root causes of the dispute and may lead to a resolution.

2. Consider bringing in a neutral third-party mediator. A mediator can help to facilitate discussions, identify common ground, and work toward a mutually acceptable solution.

3. Identify the Issues: Define the specific points of contention. Understanding the nature of the dispute is critical for reaching an agreement.

4. Seek Legal Counsel: Speak with an experienced probate or estate lawyer. They can offer legal advice, explain rights and responsibilities, and suggest possible solutions.

5. Investigate Settlement Options: Determine whether a compromise or settlement is possible. This could include asset redistribution or other negotiated terms.

6. Agreements Should Be Documented: If a resolution is reached, the terms should be clearly documented in a legally binding agreement. This will help to avoid future misunderstandings.

7. Understand Legal Rights and Responsibilities: Be aware of all parties' legal rights and responsibilities. This can be useful context for negotiations.

8. Consider Expert Opinions: When technical expertise is required (e.g., financial disputes, property valuation), seek the advice of professionals with relevant experience.

9. Maintain Deadlines and Commitments: If agreements are reached, make certain that all parties fulfill their obligations on time. This increases trust and credibility.

10. Maintain a Calm and Professional Attitude: Emotions can run high during disagreements, but keeping a calm and professional demeanor can help facilitate productive discussions.

11. Consider Arbitration or Litigation (if Necessary): If informal resolution methods fail, consider arbitration or, as a last resort, filing a lawsuit.

12. Keep an eye on legal costs: Keep an eye on the legal costs associated with resolving the dispute. It is critical to balance these costs with the potential benefits.

13. Keep detailed records of all communications, documents, and agreements related to the

dispute. These records may be useful in legal proceedings or for future reference.

14. If your first attempts at mediation were unsuccessful, consider trying again after some time has passed or if new information becomes available.

Remember that each dispute is unique, and the approach to resolution will differ depending on the circumstances. Seeking professional advice, particularly in legal matters, can be critical to protecting your rights and interests.

Litigation and Mediation
Mediation and litigation are two distinct methods of resolving disputes, each with its own set of benefits and drawbacks. Here's a rundown of both:

Mediation:

1. Process:

- Mediation involves a neutral third-party mediator who facilitates discussions between disputing parties.
- The mediator does not make decisions, but rather facilitates communication and the development of mutually acceptable solutions.

2. Participation at Will:
- Mediation is typically a voluntary process in which all parties must agree to participate.

3. Private and informal:
- Mediation proceedings are informal and private, taking place in a private setting. This frequently encourages open and honest communication.

4. Relationship Preservation:
- Because it encourages collaborative problem-solving rather than adversarial confrontation, mediation can be especially effective in preserving relationships.

5. Empowerment:

- In mediation, the parties have more say over the outcome. They actively participate in the resolution's creation, which can lead to greater satisfaction with the outcome.

6. Cost-Effective:
- Mediation can be less expensive than litigation because it typically involves fewer legal fees and a shorter time frame.

7. Flexibility:
- Mediation can resolve a wide range of disputes, from family disputes to business conflicts, and it allows for creative and tailored solutions.

Litigation:

1. Process:
- Litigation is the process of taking a legal dispute to court. The case is presided over by a judge, who makes decisions based on the applicable laws and evidence presented.

2. Adversarial and Formal:
- Litigation is a formal process that adheres to strict legal guidelines. It is a competitive process in which each party presents their case to the judge.

3. Decision that is legally binding:
- In a litigation case, the decision of the judge is legally binding on all parties involved.

4. Public Domain:
- Court proceedings and judgments are public record, which means they are open to the public.

5. Control is restricted:
- In litigation, parties have less control over the outcome because the final decision is made by the judge.

6. Potentially Expensive and Lengthy:
- Due to legal fees, court costs, and the time it takes to resolve cases through the court system, litigation can be a lengthy and costly process.

7. Suitable for Complex Cases:
- Litigation is frequently required in complex legal matters or when a party is uncooperative or non-compliant.

Finally, the decision between mediation and litigation is determined by the nature of the dispute, the preferences of the parties involved, and the facts of the case.

In some cases, a combination of both methods (mediation followed by litigation, if necessary) may be used to achieve the best possible outcome. Consultation with legal professionals can assist in determining the best approach for a specific situation.

8th Chapter

Bringing the Probate Process to a Close

To guarantee that all estate concerns are properly settled, the probate process must be completed in multiple steps. Here's a broad rule of thumb:

1. Review and Address Outstanding Debts: Before dispersing assets to heirs, make certain that all valid estate debts and expenses have been satisfied.

2. Prepare an Accounting: Provide the court with a complete accounting of the estate's assets, obligations, and transactions. As part of the probate process, this may be required.

3. Seek Court Approval (if Required): Depending on the jurisdiction and complexity of the estate, certain acts may require court

approval. This could entail assets being sold or particular bequests being distributed.

4. Final Tax Returns: Prepare and file any final tax returns required for the dead individual. This includes income taxes as well as estate taxes, if appropriate.

5. Obtain a Tax Clearance Certificate (if required): In some jurisdictions, a tax clearance certificate from the tax authorities may be required before the probate process may be completed.

6. Distribute Assets to Heirs and Beneficiaries: To distribute assets to the legitimate heirs and beneficiaries, follow the directions stated in the will or the statutes of intestate succession.

7. Maintain detailed records of all asset transfers, including dates, descriptions, and parties involved.

8. Obtain Receipts or Acknowledgements from Heirs: Request receipts or acknowledgments from heirs and beneficiaries verifying receipt of their respective assets.

9. Prepare a Final Accounting and Report: Submit to the court a final accounting and report outlining the steps completed during the probate process.

10. File a Petition for Final Distribution: In some situations, a formal petition to the court asking approval for the final distribution of assets may be required.

11. Obtain Court Approval for Final Distribution (if necessary): If the court requires approval for the final distribution, present the proper papers and seek approval from the court.

12. Close the Estate Bank Account: After all payouts and transactions have been completed, close the estate bank account.

13. Fill out a Petition for Discharge (if necessary): In some jurisdictions, the executor or administrator must file a petition with the court seeking formal discharge from their obligations.

14. Maintain Thorough Records: Keep detailed records of all acts made during the probate process, including communications, papers, and financial transactions.

15. Notify All Interested Parties: Inform all interested parties, including heirs, beneficiaries, and creditors, that the probate process has been completed.

Remember that the particular stages and regulations will differ depending on the jurisdiction and the intricacy of the estate. To ensure conformity with local rules and regulations, it is best to speak with a probate attorney or legal counselor.

Final Accounting Preparation

In the context of probate, preparing a final accounting entails producing a complete report of all financial transactions and estate-related activity. Here's a step-by-step guide:

1. Gather Financial data: Gather all necessary financial papers, such as bank statements, investment statements, receipts, invoices, and other estate-related data.

2. Organize Transactions: Arrange financial records chronologically to produce a clear and consistent timeline of all financial activity.

3. Group transactions into categories such as revenue, expenses, distributions to heirs, payments to creditors, and any other relevant classifications.

4. Include Opening and Closing Balances: Include the estate's opening balance (the value of assets at the start of the probate process) and closing balance (the value at the completion of the process).

5. Detail Each Transaction: Provide the date, description, amount, and persons involved for each transaction. Payments made, costs incurred, and money received are all included.

6. Summarize Each Category: To provide a comprehensive summary of the financial activity, calculate the total amount for each category.

7. Attach copies of necessary papers, such as invoices, receipts, contracts, or legal letters, to substantiate the recorded transactions.

8. Verify Accuracy: Check all entries for accuracy and make sure all financial data is included.

9. Prepare a Written Report: Write a detailed narrative outlining the estate's financial actions. This should include a synopsis of the transactions, any odd or notable events, and any

difficulties encountered during the probate process.

10. Provide an Explanation for Discrepancies: If there are any discrepancies or unexpected transactions, explain them clearly.

11. Final Accounting manner: Arrange the final accounting in a professional and easy-to-read manner. For a sophisticated presentation, consider employing spreadsheet software or accounting software.

12. Obtain Required Signatures (if Applicable): If the final accounting requires approval from the court or other interested parties, ensure that the required signatures are obtained.

13. Distribute to Interested Parties: Distribute final accounting copies to all relevant parties, including heirs, beneficiaries, and any court-appointed officials managing the probate process.

14. Keep Records: For your personal records, keep copies of the final accounting and all supporting documentation. These may be needed in the future for reference or auditing.

15. Seek Professional Advice (if Necessary): If you're unsure about any aspect of the final accounting, seek advice from a probate attorney or financial advisor.

Keep in mind that the final accounting should be accurate, open, and thorough. It acts as a vital record of the estate's financial activity and maintains legal compliance.

Estate Administration

Closing an estate entails completing the legal and administrative processes required to properly end the probate process. Here's a general guide to getting started:

1. Verify Probate Process Completion: Ensure that all necessary procedures of the probate

process, such as settling outstanding bills, distributing assets, and producing a final accounting, have been completed.

2. Obtain Court consent (if Required): Before officially closing the estate, you may need to obtain court consent in specific situations. This may entail submitting a petition or supplying documentation.

3. Pay any outstanding bills, charges, or obligations linked with the estate, including legal fees, administrative costs, and outstanding debts.

4. Prepare and file any final tax returns for the deceased person, including income taxes and, if appropriate, estate taxes.

5. Obtain a Tax Clearance Certificate (if required): In some jurisdictions, a tax clearance certificate from the tax authorities may be required before closing the estate.

6. Prepare a Final Accounting and Report: Submit to the court a final accounting and report detailing all acts made during the probate process. This document may be required by the court.

7. File a Petition for Final Distribution (if necessary): If the final distribution of assets requires court approval, file the necessary petition and seek the court's approval.

8. Distribute Remaining Assets: Ensure that all remaining assets are allocated to the legitimate heirs and beneficiaries in accordance with the terms of the will or the laws of intestate succession.

9. Obtain Receipts or Acknowledgements from Heirs: Obtain receipts or acknowledgements from heirs and beneficiaries to certify receipt of their respective assets.

10. Close the Estate Bank Account: After all payouts and transactions have been completed, close the estate bank account.

11. Fill out a Petition for Discharge (if necessary): In some jurisdictions, the executor or administrator must file a petition with the court seeking formal discharge from their obligations.

12. Notify All Interested Parties: Inform all interested parties, including heirs, beneficiaries, and creditors, that the probate process has been completed.

13. Maintain Thorough Records: Keep detailed records of all acts made during the probate process, including communications, papers, and financial transactions.

14. File a Closing Statement (if required): To officially close the estate, you may be required to file a closing statement with the court in some jurisdictions.

15. Distribute Final Accountings: Make copies of the final accounting and accompanying papers for the records of all interested parties.

Remember that the particular stages and regulations will differ depending on the jurisdiction and the intricacy of the estate. To ensure conformity with local rules and regulations, it is best to speak with a probate attorney or legal counselor.

Disbursement of Remaining Assets

The final step in distributing residual assets is to transfer the remaining property, goods, and cash resources to the rightful heirs and beneficiaries. Here's how you can do it:

1. Create an inventory of any remaining assets, including real estate, personal property, financial accounts, investments, and any other valuable objects.

2. Check Legal Authority: Make sure you have the legal authority to disperse the assets. This usually entails being designated as the executor or administrator of the estate via the probate process.

3. Examine the Will (if applicable): If there is a will, thoroughly read it to understand the deceased person's desires for asset distribution. The will should include clear instructions on who should receive what.

4. Be aware of any legal requirements or limits that may apply to the distribution of specific types of assets. Real estate transfers, for example, may necessitate specific documentation.

5. Consider Outstanding Debts and Expenses: Before distributing assets, ensure that all lawful debts and expenses of the estate have been satisfied. Funeral expenses, taxes, and any other outstanding debts may be included.

6. Inform Heirs and Beneficiaries: Notify the heirs and beneficiaries of the planned distribution. Give them a precise timeframe and directions on how to carry out the process.

7. Obtain Acknowledgements or Receipts: Request receipts or acknowledgments from heirs and beneficiaries proving receipt of their respective assets. This aids in keeping a clear record of the distribution.

8. Use Fair and Transparent Methods: When it comes to asset allocation, be fair and transparent. Treat all heirs and beneficiaries fairly and objectively.

9. Consider Personal Property: If several heirs are interested in certain items of personal property (e.g., jewelry, heirlooms), consider devising a fair process for sharing or distributing these assets.

10. Address Special Bequests (if any): If the will provides specific bequests (gifts) to persons or

organizations, ensure that they are dispersed in the manner specified.

11. Maintain Thorough Records: Keep detailed records of all distributions, including asset descriptions, names of recipients, and dates of transfer. This documentation is necessary for legal and accounting reasons.

12. Consider Tax Implications: Be mindful of any tax consequences related with the distribution of certain assets, such as capital gains taxes on the sale of real estate.

13. Close Accounts and Update Titles: If necessary, close accounts in the dead person's name, such as bank or utility accounts. Real estate and automobile titles and ownership data should be updated.

14. Document the Distribution Process: Create a final report or statement that summarizes the asset distribution. This paper can be used as a formal record of the procedure.

15. Seek Professional Advice (if Necessary): Consult with a probate attorney or legal counsel if you are unsure about any part of distributing specific assets or if there are significant legal implications.

Remember to follow all legal procedures and thoroughly document the distribution process to verify that the distribution is carried out in accordance with the law and the deceased person's desires.

9th Chapter

Special Rules for Heirs and Beneficiaries

Certain specific issues may arise when dispersing assets to heirs and beneficiaries. Here are some crucial items to remember:

1. Equal Treatment: Unless there are specific provisions in the will that state otherwise, treat all heirs and beneficiaries fairly and equitably.

2. Specific Bequests: Take careful note of any specific bequests included in the will. These are instructions for distributing specified products or sums to certain people or organizations.

3. Personal things such as jewelry, artwork, and family heirlooms may have sentimental value. Consider how these products will be divided, and if necessary, create a fair decision-making procedure.

4. Real estate transfers can be complicated both legally and logistically. Check that all relevant documents and processes are followed, and think about any tax implications.

5. Financial Assets: When distributing financial assets such as bank accounts, investments, and retirement accounts, account ownership and beneficiary designations must be carefully considered.

6. Minor Beneficiaries: If a beneficiary is under the age of 18, consider establishing a trust or other structure to manage their inheritance until they reach the legal age of majority.

7. Beneficiaries with Special Needs: Beneficiaries with special needs may require extra planning to ensure that their inheritance does not affect their eligibility for government support programs.

8. Consider the potential tax implications for both the estate and the beneficiaries. Different sorts of assets may be taxed differently.

9. bills and fees: Before distributing assets to heirs and beneficiaries, make sure that any outstanding bills, such as funeral fees, taxes, and administrative costs, are settled.

10. Maintain open and transparent communication with your heirs and beneficiaries. Explain the method, timeline, and any specific factors that may be applicable.

11. Minor Guardianship: If a minor is specified as a beneficiary, consider naming a guardian to look after their financial interests until they reach the age of majority.

12. If charitable organizations are mentioned as beneficiaries, be certain that their assigned share is allocated accurately and in accordance with the will.

13. Contingent Beneficiaries: You should be aware of any contingent beneficiaries specified in the will. If the primary beneficiaries are unable to inherit assets, these individuals or entities will.

14. Documentation and recordkeeping: Keep detailed records of all distributions, including asset descriptions, names of recipients, and dates of transfer. This documentation is necessary for legal and accounting reasons.

15. Seek Professional Advice: When dealing with difficult or delicate cases, such as those involving special needs beneficiaries or large sums of money, it's best to consult with a knowledgeable probate attorney or financial counselor.

Remember that each situation is unique, and the specific issues will rely on the estate's and its recipients' individual circumstances. Taking the time to thoroughly address these factors will assist ensure a smooth and equitable distribution process.

Spousal Support

Spousal rights are the legal rights and safeguards granted to a surviving spouse throughout an estate or probate process. These rights may differ depending on the jurisdiction and the specifics of the marriage. Here are some examples of common spousal rights:

1. Right to Inherit: A surviving spouse has the right to inherit a share of the deceased spouse's inheritance even if there is no will (intestate succession) in many jurisdictions. The precise share may differ depending on local legislation.

2. Elective Share: Some jurisdictions have rules that allow a surviving spouse to choose a statutory share over the provisions of the deceased spouse's will. This assures that the surviving spouse receives a proportionate share of the estate.

3. Homestead Exemption: Under the homestead exemption, a surviving spouse may be able to continue residing in the family home for a set amount of time, or in some situations indefinitely.

4. Family Allowance: In some countries, a specified amount of money is set aside for the support of the surviving spouse and any dependent children.

5. Dower and curtsey rights: In the past, some countries recognized dower (for widows) and curtsey (for widowers) rights, which gave a surviving spouse a life interest in specific real property.

6. Exempt Property: In some circumstances, a surviving spouse may be able to claim certain property, such as domestic furnishings or personal effects, as exempt from creditors' claims.

7. Spousal Support or Maintenance: If a surviving spouse was financially reliant on the deceased spouse, they may be entitled to spousal support or maintenance from the deceased spouse's estate.

8. Medical Decision-Making: If no advance directives or powers of attorney were in place, a surviving spouse may have legal ability to make medical decisions on behalf of the deceased spouse.

9. Funeral and Burial Decisions: Typically, a surviving spouse has the ability to make decisions regarding the deceased's funeral and burial arrangements.

10. Right to Administer the Estate: A surviving spouse may be appointed as the executor or administrator of the estate of the deceased spouse first.

11. Prenuptial and Postnuptial Agreements: Any prenuptial or postnuptial agreements entered into

between the couples can have an impact on spousal rights.

It's crucial to note that the precise rights of a surviving spouse can be influenced by a variety of factors, including the length of the marriage, the presence of children, and any legal agreements or papers that were made (such as wills or trusts). Spousal rights laws and regulations differ by jurisdiction, so it's best to contact a skilled attorney for counsel tailored to your individual circumstances.

Children's and Other Beneficiaries' Rights

Children and other beneficiaries have special rights and safeguards, especially during an estate or probate process. Here are some examples of common rights:

1. Children and other beneficiaries designated in a will or decided by law (in circumstances of intestacy) have a legal right to inherit assets from a deceased person's estate.

2. Disinheritance Protection: Most jurisdictions have regulations in place to prevent parents from entirely disinheriting their children. Even if they are not named in a will, children may be entitled to a piece of the estate.

3. Beneficiaries are typically entitled to equal treatment, unless there are particular provisions in the will that require otherwise.

4. Beneficiaries have the right to be informed about the probate procedure, including obtaining notice of court proceedings and updates on the estate's status.

5. Beneficiaries have the right to challenge the validity of a will if they believe it was obtained by coercion, fraud, or undue influence.

6. Beneficiaries have the right to request and receive from the executor or administrator an accounting of the estate's assets, liabilities, and transactions.

7. Right to Challenge the Executor's Actions: If a beneficiary believes that the executor or administrator is not acting in the best interests of the estate, they have the right to sue.

8. Beneficiaries have the right to receive their individual parts of the remaining assets once the estate's debts and liabilities have been settled.

9. Protection of Minor Beneficiaries: When a minor is identified as a beneficiary, certain legal safeguards are generally in place to ensure that their rights are safeguarded until they reach the age of majority.

10. Beneficiary Designations: Beneficiaries named on assets such as life insurance policies, retirement funds, and payable-on-death accounts have the right to claim the proceeds.

11. Special Bequests: Beneficiaries have the right to be informed if the will includes special bequests (gifts) to them.

12. Right to Contest Undue Influence or Fraud: A beneficiary has the right to contest the validity of a will if they believe it was written under duress or via fraud.

13. Beneficiaries have the right to assume that some components of the probate procedure, including sensitive personal information, will be kept confidential.

14. Asset Valuation Contestation: Beneficiaries have the right to contest asset valuations if they believe they are being undervalued or overpriced.

Beneficiaries' rights can differ depending on jurisdiction and the unique conditions of the estate. A knowledgeable probate attorney can provide specialized guidance depending on the specific situation.

Trusts and Their Function

A trust is a legal structure in which one party (the settlor or grantor) distributes property or assets to another (the trustee) for the benefit of a third party or parties (the beneficiaries). Trusts serve numerous functions in estate planning and asset management:

1. Asset Protection: Trusts can shield assets against creditors, lawsuits, and other potential threats. This is especially useful for high-net-worth individuals or those in professions with a high liability risk.

2. Estate Planning: Trusts are an effective tool for controlling the distribution of assets following the death of the settlor. They can assist in avoiding or minimizing the probate process, resulting in a smoother transfer of assets to beneficiaries.

3. Privacy: Unlike wills, which become public record when filed with the court, trusts can often give more privacy because they do not have to be recorded publicly.

4. Control and Flexibility: The settlor has complete control over how the assets in the trust are managed and distributed. This can contain distribution conditions, particular purposes (such as education or medical bills), and timetables.

5. Managing Assets for Minors or Incapacitated People: Trusts can keep and manage assets for minors or people who are unable to manage their own affairs. This guarantees that their financial demands are met in a prudent manner.

6. Avoiding Probate: Assets kept in trust are often not subject to the probate process, which may be time-consuming, expensive, and public. This facilitates the transfer of assets to recipients.

7. Tax Efficiency: Certain trusts, such as irrevocable trusts, can be utilized for estate tax planning, potentially lowering the estate's overall tax liability.

8. Charitable Giving: Through charitable trusts, individuals can assist their favorite charities while potentially benefiting from tax breaks. These trusts can provide an income stream to the donor or beneficiaries while also benefiting the nonprofit organization of choice.

9. Trusts can be used to help enable the smooth transfer of ownership and control of a family business to the next generation.

10. Special Needs Trusts: Special needs trusts are intended to give financial help to people with disabilities while maintaining their eligibility for government assistance programs.

11. Avoiding Family Disputes: The settlor can help avoid potential conflicts among beneficiaries or other interested parties by providing explicit instructions in the trust document.

12. Long-Term Financial Planning: Trusts can be utilized as part of a complete financial plan to

ensure that assets are managed prudently and that their usage and distribution are organized.

It is crucial to realize that there are numerous sorts of trusts, each with its own set of aims and benefits. The particular sort of trust and its provisions will be determined by the settlor's own goals and circumstances. Consultation with an expert estate planning attorney or financial advisor is required to create a trust that meets your individual goals.

10th Chapter

The Most Common Mistakes and How to Avoid Them

The estate planning and probate procedure can be complicated, and there are several common mistakes that people may face. Here are some of these dangers, as well as tips on how to prevent them:

Lack of a Will or Estate Plan:
- Pitfall: Failure to make a will or prepare an estate plan might lead to uncertainty and potential conflicts over asset distribution.
- Avoidance: Work with an estate planning professional to draft a detailed will or trust that represents your wishes.

2. Failure to Keep Estate Documents Up to Date:
- Pitfall: Failure to amend your will or trust to reflect significant life changes (e.g., marriage,

divorce, childbirth) might result in out-of-date instructions.

- Avoidance: Review and amend your estate documents on a regular basis, particularly following important life events.

3. Neglecting Digital Assets:
- Pitfall: Failure to include digital assets (e.g., online accounts, cryptocurrencies) in your estate plan can make them difficult to access or transfer.
- Avoidance: Include provisions in your estate plan for digital assets, detailing how they should be handled or dispersed.

4. Not Considering Tax Consequences:
- Pitfall: Failure to grasp the tax implications of estate planning decisions might result in tax liabilities for beneficiaries that are unnecessary.
- Avoidance: Work with a tax expert or estate planning attorney to create tax-avoidance measures.

5. Failure to Name Beneficiaries on Accounts:

- Pitfall: Failure to designate beneficiaries on assets such as retirement accounts and life insurance policies may result in distribution delays and problems.
- Avoidance: Review and amend beneficiary designations on a regular basis to ensure they reflect your current objectives.

6. Documentation or records that are incomplete:
- Pitfall: Inadequate documentation can cause misunderstanding or disagreements during the probate process.
- Prevention: Keep detailed and organized records of all estate-related papers, such as wills, trusts, financial statements, and account information.

7. Not Taking Special Circumstances into Account:
- Pitfall: Failure to account for beneficiaries with special needs, minor children, or complex family dynamics might result in unforeseen effects.

- Avoidance: Consult with a special needs planning attorney and examine the unique needs of your beneficiaries.

8. Selecting the Incorrect Executor or Trustee:
- Pitfall: Appointing an executor or trustee who is unprepared or unwilling to carry out their duties can result in problems.
- Avoidance: Choose people who are trustworthy, capable, and willing to take on the task, and clearly convey your aims.

9. Missing Health Care Directives:
- Pitfall: Failure to create advance directives for healthcare decisions might lead to family members being confused and disagreeing.
- Prevention: Create a healthcare power of attorney and a living will to ensure that your medical wishes are understood and followed.

10. Not Seeking Professional Help:
- Pitfall: Attempting to negotiate complex estate planning or probate matters without the

assistance of an expert might result in costly mistakes.

- Avoidance: Seek the advice of competent estate planning attorneys, financial consultants, and tax professionals to ensure your plan is well-structured and legally solid.

Avoiding these typical hazards requires careful preparation, regular updates, and the use of expert counsel when necessary. Consulting with estate planning and probate professionals can assist you in developing a comprehensive strategy that matches with your aims and protects your interests.

Potential Difficulties

There are various possible issues that can develop during the estate planning and probate process. It is critical to be aware of these and plan accordingly. Here are some potential difficulties and solutions:

1. Disputes Between Heirs:

- Difficulty: Heirs may have opposing views on how assets should be allocated, which could lead to conflicts or legal issues.
- Address: Clear directions in the estate plan, as well as mediation or legal action, can assist resolve disagreements.

2. Family Dynamics that are Complicated:
- Difficulty: Complicated family ties, blended families, or alienated relatives can also complicate asset distribution.
- Address: To establish a plan that accommodates complex family relationships, clearly articulate your desires, consider unique provisions, and speak with an experienced estate planning attorney.

3. Beneficiaries with Special Needs:
- Difficulty: Providing for individuals with special needs necessitates careful planning to ensure they receive the appropriate assistance while remaining eligible for government assistance programs.

- Address: Create a special needs trust and consult with an attorney versed in special needs planning to develop a plan that addresses the beneficiaries' unique needs.

4. Tax Obligations:
- Obstacle: Taxes, such as estate taxes, capital gains taxes, and income taxes, can have a considerable impact on the value of assets passed down to heirs.
- Address: Collaborate with a tax advisor and an estate planning attorney to develop methods that reduce tax exposure while achieving your objectives.

5. Managing Commercial Interests:
- Difficulty: Handing down a family business or managing business holdings inside an estate necessitates careful planning to assure continuity and resolve potential heir conflicts.
- Address: Think about succession planning, buy-sell agreements, and consulting with business and estate planning experts.

6. Real Estate Management:
- Difficulty: Managing and distributing real estate holdings can be difficult, especially if there are many properties or properties in different jurisdictions.
- Address: Collaborate with a real estate specialist and an attorney to create a strategy for managing and distributing real estate assets.

7. Claims of Creditors:
Creditors may file claims against the estate, thus limiting the amount available for distribution to heirs and beneficiaries.
- Address: Identify and settle valid debts in a timely manner while according to legal procedures, and contact with an attorney if disagreements develop.

8. Documentation that is out of date:
- Problem: Outdated or inadequate estate paperwork might cause confusion and disagreements among heirs.

- Address: Review and update your estate plan on a regular basis to reflect changes in your circumstances, assets, and wishes.

9. Instructions or intentions that are unclear:
- Difficulty: Ambiguities or a lack of clarity in the estate plan might cause misunderstanding and disagreements among beneficiaries.
- Address: Make your wishes clear in your estate documents and get legal counsel to guarantee they are legally enforceable and unambiguous.

10. Keeping Unintended Consequences at Bay:
- Difficulty: When dealing with complex financial arrangements or familial situations, the unintended implications of some planning decisions can develop.
- Address: Seek professional counsel from estate planning attorneys, financial advisors, and tax professionals to fully understand the implications of your selections.

Addressing these possible issues requires careful planning, clear communication, and the assistance of skilled professionals. A well-structured estate plan, prepared with a grasp of potential challenges, can assist your heirs and beneficiaries have a more pleasant experience.

Executor Best Practices

Being an executor entails a great deal of duty. Here are some recommended practices to help you carry out your responsibilities effectively:

1. Recognize Your Role and Responsibilities:
- Learn about the legal and financial responsibilities of an executor in your jurisdiction.

2. Keep Communication Open:
- Inform beneficiaries and interested parties of significant developments and decisions.

3. Organize and record everything:
- Keep meticulous records of all estate transactions, communications, and decisions.

4. Seek Professional Help When Necessary:
- Seek advice from specialists such as attorneys, accountants, or financial consultants on complex issues.

5. Put safety and security first:
- Protect critical valuables and important documents from loss or theft.

6. Set reasonable expectations:
- Be open and honest with beneficiaries regarding timelines and the difficulties of the process.

7. Manage Estate Assets With Care:
- Oversee and preserve assets, ensuring proper maintenance and management.

8. Pay off debts and liabilities as soon as possible:
- Pay the estate's legitimate debts and costs on promptly.

9. Maintain your objectivity and fairness:

- Give equal consideration to all beneficiaries and eliminate conflicts of interest.

10. Observe Legal Requirements:
- Comply with all probate-related local laws, regulations, and court orders.

11. Timely submission of required documents:
- Submit required papers, such as inventories and accountings, within the deadline.

12. Address Tax Issues Wisely:
- Make certain that all required tax returns and filings are filed correctly and on time.

13. Avoid Merging Funds:
- To maintain openness and accountability, keep estate money separate from your personal accounts.

14. Keep Beneficiaries Up to Date on Progress:
- Inform beneficiaries on the status of the probate process and any noteworthy developments on a regular basis.

15. Seek Court Approval as Needed:
- As needed by law, obtain court permission for substantial transactions or payouts.

16. Diplomatic Resolution of Disputes and Conflicts:
- If disagreements emerge, try to resolve them by open conversation, mediation, or, if necessary, legal action.

17. Thoroughly document your actions:
- Keep accurate records of all actions, including dates, descriptions, and persons involved.

18. Keep Professionalism and Integrity:
- Carry out your responsibilities with honesty, integrity, and in accordance with legal and ethical norms.

19. Distribute Assets Equitably and Consistently with the Will:
- For asset distribution, follow the directions in the will or the statutes of intestate succession.

20. Obtain Heirs' Receipts or Acknowledgements:
- Request receipts or acknowledgments from heirs and beneficiaries proving receipt of their respective assets.

Remember that being an executor can be a difficult job. Seek expert assistance, communicate honestly with beneficiaries, and make certain that all measures are taken in the best interests of the estate and its beneficiaries. If you have any questions concerning your role, consult with a knowledgeable attorney.

11th Chapter

Finishing the Probate Process

Finishing the probate process entails completing the final processes to officially finish the estate administration. Here's a checklist to help you get through this crucial stage:

1. Verify Probate Process Completion: Ensure that all necessary procedures of the probate process, such as settling outstanding bills, distributing assets, and producing a final accounting, have been completed.

2. Obtain Court Approval (if relevant): If court approval is required to close the estate, file the relevant paperwork and seek court approval.

3. Pay any outstanding bills, charges, or obligations linked with the estate, including legal fees, administrative costs, and outstanding debts.

4. Prepare and file any final tax returns for the deceased person, including income taxes and, if appropriate, estate taxes.

5. Obtain a Tax Clearance Certificate (if required): In some jurisdictions, a tax clearance certificate from the tax authorities may be required before closing the estate.

6. Prepare a Final Accounting and Report: Submit to the court a final accounting and report detailing all acts made during the probate process. This document may be required by the court.

7. File a Petition for Final Distribution (if necessary): If the final distribution of assets requires court approval, file the necessary petition and seek the court's approval.

8. Distribute Remaining Assets: Ensure that all remaining assets are allocated to the legitimate heirs and beneficiaries in accordance with the

terms of the will or the laws of intestate succession.

9. Obtain Receipts or Acknowledgements from Heirs: Obtain receipts or acknowledgements from heirs and beneficiaries to certify receipt of their respective assets.

10. Close the Estate Bank Account: After all payouts and transactions have been completed, close the estate bank account.

11. In some countries, you may be obliged to file a petition with the court seeking formal dismissal from your duties as executor.

12. Notify All Interested Parties: Inform all interested parties, including heirs, beneficiaries, and creditors, that the probate process has been completed.

13. Maintain Thorough Records: Keep detailed records of all acts made during the probate

process, including communications, papers, and financial transactions.

14. File a Closing Statement (if required): To officially close the estate, you may be required to file a closing statement with the court in some jurisdictions.

15. Distribute Final Accountings: Make copies of the final accounting and accompanying papers for the records of all interested parties.

Remember that the particular stages and regulations will differ depending on the jurisdiction and the intricacy of the estate. To ensure conformity with local rules and regulations, it is best to speak with a probate attorney or legal counselor. You can successfully complete the probate process by following this checklist and receiving expert assistance if needed.

Moving On After Probate

Following probate, many critical measures must be taken to close the estate and settle any outstanding issues. Here's a guide to help you get through this stage:

1. Confirm Probate Process Completion: Ensure that all necessary elements of the probate process, such as debt settlement, asset distribution, and gaining court approval, have been completed successfully.

2. Notify All Interested Parties: Inform all interested parties, including heirs, beneficiaries, and creditors, that the probate process has concluded.

3. Maintain Thorough Records: Keep detailed records of all acts made during the probate process, including communications, papers, and financial transactions. These documents are necessary for legal and accounting purposes.

4. To officially close the estate, you may need to file closing documentation with the court or

other applicable authorities, depending on your jurisdiction.

5. Distribute Final Accountings: Make copies of the final accounting and accompanying papers for the records of all interested parties.

6. Complete Tax Obligations:
- Prepare and file any final tax returns for the deceased individual, including income and estate taxes, if applicable.
- Obtain any tax clearance certificates that are required.

7. Close Estate Bank Account: After all payouts and transactions have been completed, close the estate bank account.

8. Address Any Remaining bills or costs: Ensure that the estate's legitimate bills and costs have been satisfied.

9. Finalize Special Bequests (if any): If the will includes special bequests (gifts), make sure they are disbursed in the manner specified.

10. Protect your property and assets:
- If any assets or properties remain, ensure they are adequately secured and maintained.

11. Unsold Asset Disposal (if applicable): Determine the best course of action for disposing of unsold assets, whether through sale or other means.

12. Legal and financial documents should be updated:
- Review and update your personal legal and financial records in light of any changes that may occur as a result of the probate process.

13. Inform the following institutions and authorities:
- Notify banks, financial institutions, and relevant government organizations that the probate process has been completed.

14. Think about Grief and Emotional Support:
- Recognize that the probate process can be emotionally taxing. If necessary, seek help from friends, family, or professional counselors.

15. Consult with Experts for Future Planning:
- If you are a beneficiary, talk to an estate planning attorney or a financial expert about how to plan for your own future.

16. Maintain Consistent Contact with Beneficiaries:
- Keep beneficiaries up to date on any outstanding issues and confirm that they have received their appropriate assets.

17. Make a record of the procedure:
- Maintain a detailed record of all steps made during the probate process.

Following these steps will ensure a smooth transfer out of probate and into the next phase.

Remember that expert guidance from an attorney or financial advisor can be invaluable in making informed decisions and ensuring legal compliance.

Printed in Great Britain
by Amazon

36425438R00086